Succeeding with the Masters®
& The Festival Collection®
ETUDES with Technique

About the Series

This series is designed to develop healthy, natural, and effective technique so that students can play beautifully as well as with virtuosity. Each book is divided into units and each unit focuses on one technical concept. Technical concepts are introduced using imagery to help the student understand the gesture needed to produce the correct technique. Following the text and the imagery, two short technical exercises provide the student's first opportunity to play the technique. These exercises should be memorized so students can focus on the sound they produce while observing their playing mechanism in action. Several etudes then follow to reinforce each technical concept. In this way, students focus on one technique at a time, and the concept is reinforced through multiple etudes. This method allows the student to master the technique and make it a habit, providing the foundation for effective, natural, relaxed, and enjoyable performances of their repertoire.

The student should concentrate on looking at being aware of the feeling in their fingers and fingertips, hands, wrists, forearms, elbows, and upper arms in order to produce the correct gestures. In order to achieve a fluid and solid technique, students must always listen carefully to themselves and the sound they create.

This series is best used with the following curriculum:

Etudes with Technique, Preparatory = The Festival Collection®, Preparatory = Succeeding at the Piano, Grade 2A

Etudes with Technique, Book 1 = The Festival Collection®, Book 1 = On Your Way to Succeeding with the Masters® = Succeeding at the Piano™, Grade 2B

Etudes with Technique, Book 2 = The Festival Collection®, Book 2 = An Introduction to Succeeding with the Masters® = Succeeding with the Masters®, Volume One = Succeeding at the Piano™, Grade 3A

THE
F·J·H
MUSIC
COMPANY
IN C.
Frank J. Hackinson

Production: Frank J. Hackinson
Production Coordinator: Joyce Loke and Satish Bhakta
Cover Art Concept: Helen Marlais
Cover Design: Terpstra Design, San Francisco, CA
Illustration: Keith Criss, TradigitalWorks, Oakland, CA
Engraving: Tempo Music Press, Inc.
Printer: Tempo Music Press, Inc.

ISBN-13: 978-1-56939-831-9

Etudes with Technique, Preparatory

Practice Tips

An etude is a piece that is written to help students master an instrument, or practice a technique. For all of the units in this series, practice in the following ways:

1. Read over the text and the imagery for each technical concept. Then practice the technical exercises. Memorizing these short patterns will keep you focused on two important goals: achieving the best sound; and observing what your fingers, hands, wrists, forearms, elbows, upper arms, and shoulders are doing!

2. There is a helpful Practice Strategy above each etude to guide you in practicing or interpreting each etude.

3. Look over the entire etude to discover its patterns and the main technical concept that the etude addresses.

4. Practice the etude as you would repertoire pieces—with attention to detail, in short sections, isolating trouble spots, and hands-separate practice.

5. Once you learn the piece, practice it at different tempos. Always listen for a beautiful sound in your playing.

6. Remember to keep your shoulders low and wide, relaxed, and sit tall at the bench.

    Reviewing units often is an excellent way to establish a strong technical foundation. You will find that by going back to a unit after a period of time, that unit will be much easier to play the second time and reviewing it will confirm your technical mastery!

4

Etudes with Technique, Preparatory

Composer	Title	Theme	Page

FJH2024

Progress Log

Unit	Piece	Date Started	Date Finished
1	**Melodic Intervals**, p. 7		
	Etude (*Variation 3*), p. 8		
	Etude (*Variation 6*), p. 8		
	Etude (*Op. 82, No. 7*), p. 9		
	Two Panda Bears, p. 10		
	Playful Porpoise, p. 10		
2	**Harmonic Intervals**, p. 11		
	Etude No. 5, p. 12		
	Making Cartwheels, p. 12		
	Marching Tune, p. 13		
	The Bird's First Song, p. 13		
	Little Arabesque, p. 14		
	Etude (*Op. 823, No. 8*), p. 14		
3	**Five-Finger Patterns**, p. 15		
	Etude (*Variation 11*), p. 16		
	Etude (*Variation 12*), p. 16		
	Etude, p. 17		
	Etude (*Op. 82, No. 8*), p. 17		
4	**Two Friends Walking**, p. 18		
	Etude (*Op. 82, No. 12*), p. 19		
	Etude (*Op. 101, No. 22*), p. 19		
	Four Etudes, p. 20		
	Canon in F (*Op. 14, No. 9*), p. 21		
	Prairie Moon, p. 22		

Unit 1 - Melodic Intervals

A melody is a string of notes that make a tune. Melodic intervals form a melody, one note at a time. Imagine that a melody is a string of pearls, with each note being round and beautiful, like a pearl. Listen for each note to lead to the next one.

Play and sing the melodies below. Notice the 2nd, 3rd, 4th, and 5th intervals.

Scarborough Fair

Traditional

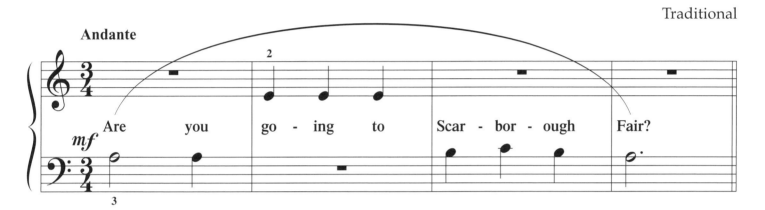

Andante

mf Are you go - ing to Scar - bor - ough Fair?

She'll Be Comin' 'round the Mountain

Traditional

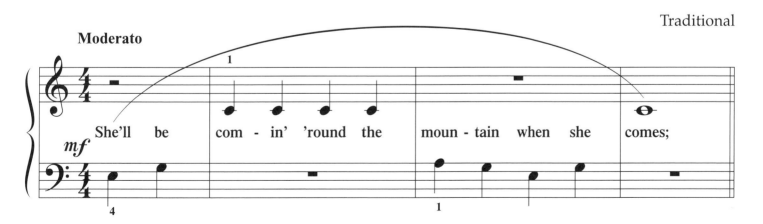

Moderato

mf She'll be com - in' 'round the moun - tain when she comes;

ETUDE

from *The Elementary Instruction Book, Variation 3*

Ferdinand Beyer
(1803-1863)

- Listen carefully for the two- and three-note slurs.

Transpose to: C major_____

D major_____

ETUDE

from *The Elementary Instruction Book, Variation 6*

Ferdinand Beyer
(1803-1863)

- Transfer the weight of your arm from one finger to the next, letting your wrist roll in one smooth motion.

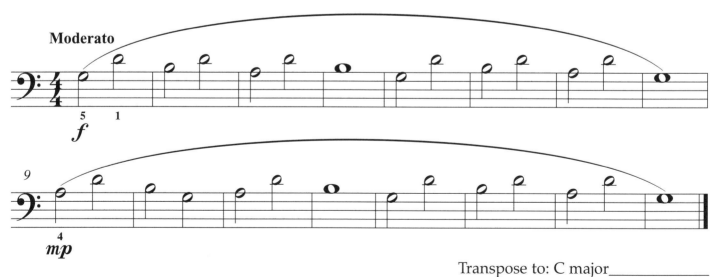

Transpose to: C major_____

D major_____

Other Keys:_____

ETUDE

from *The First Steps of the Young Pianist, Opus 82, No. 7*

Cornelius Gurlitt
(1820-1901)

- The two etudes below are similar since they use the same notes.
  Notice the first one is *legato,* and the second one is *staccato.*
  How else are they different?
- Plan the melodic intervals before playing.

Allegro

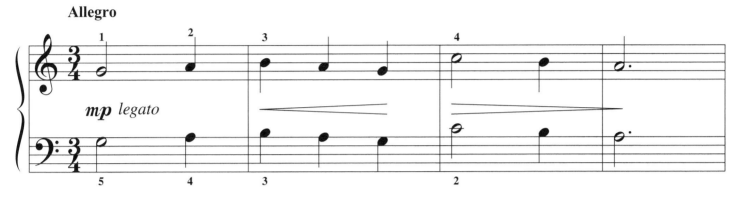

Moderato

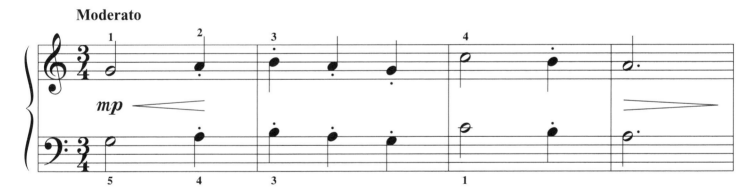

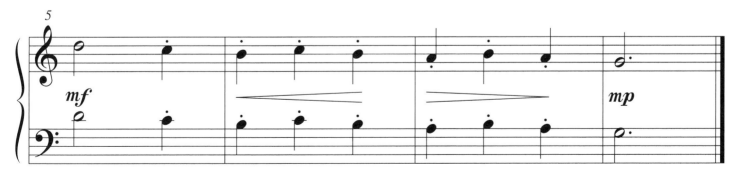

Can you play these etudes in D major?_____yes, no

C major?_____yes, no

Other Keys:_____

Two Panda Bears

• Listen carefully for eveness as well as dynamics.

Helen Marlais
(1965-   )

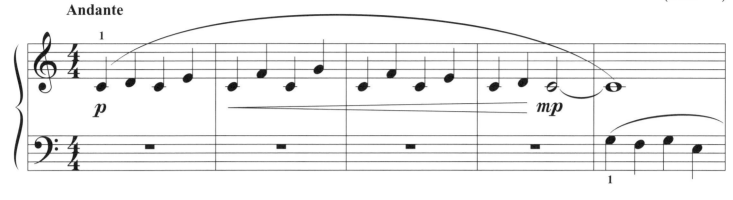

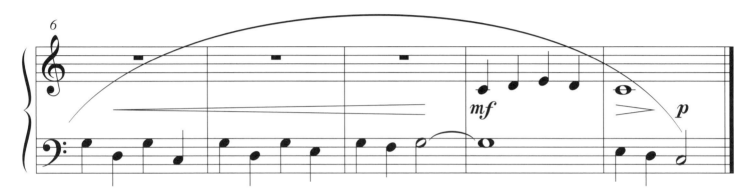

Playful Porpoise

Helen Marlais
(1965-   )

• Listen and count so that each three-note slur is steady.

Unit 2 - Harmonic Intervals

Harmonic intervals are when two notes are played together. This sound of two notes together creates the harmony. Harmonic intervals on the musical staff are notes that are stacked vertically. Think of the melody (melodic intervals) as jam, and the harmony (made up of harmonic intervals) as bread. The melody needs to be louder than the harmony in order to make music sound good!

• When you play the melody in the right hand, transfer the weight of your arm behind each finger as it plays. You will achieve a beautiful sound in this way, without reaching for any keys.

• When you play the *harmonic* intervals in your left hand, notice that your arm feels lighter than the right hand. Play lightly on your fingertips for a crisp, *staccato* sound.

Helen Marlais

Etude No. 5

Johann Christian Bach (1735-1782)
Francesco Pasquale Ricci (1732-1817)

• Let your wrist and forearm play as one unit for each harmonic third.

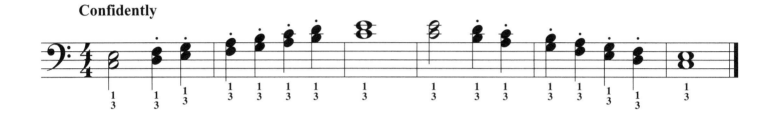

Making Cartwheels

Helen Marlais
(1965-   )

• Block (play together) all the intervals of a 5th in each measure. When you play as written, start on the key and spring up for each *staccato*.

Marching Tune

• For the etudes on this page, listen for the balance between the right and left hands.

Timothy Brown
(1959-   )

Moderato

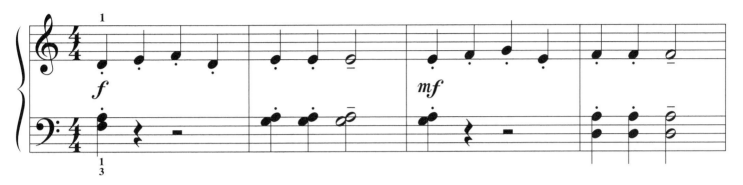

The Bird's First Song

Timothy Brown
(1959-   )

Moderato

FJH2024

LITTLE ARABESQUE

Valerie Roth Roubos
(1955-   )

- Where are the harmonic intervals?
- Listen for smooth playing in both hands.

Moderato

ETUDE

from *The Little Pianist, Opus 823, No. 8*

Carl Czerny
(1791-1857)

- Practice the harmonic intervals first. While playing them, shift your weight as you change from a third to a fifth interval. When comfortable, add the right hand.

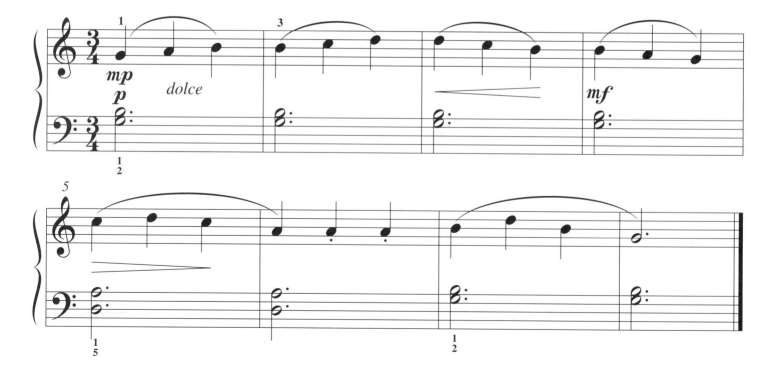

Unit 3 - Five-Finger Patterns

Let your wrists and arms be flexible when playing five-finger patterns. When playing each note of a five-finger pattern in the right hand, your wrist, arm, and elbow move together. Imagine that your arm is a wave, moving away from the shore. Your wrist and arm will move down and then around to the right. Then they will continue to move around and up, like a wave in the air. Lastly, the wave crests, on its way back to shore.

Your left hand will move the same way when playing the following exercise.

Helen Marlais

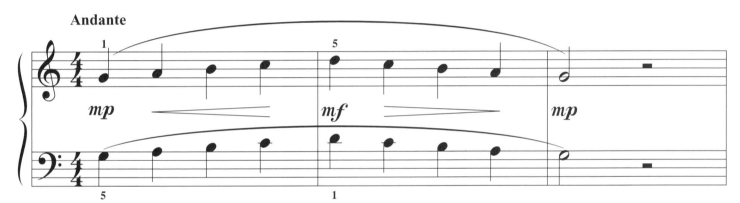

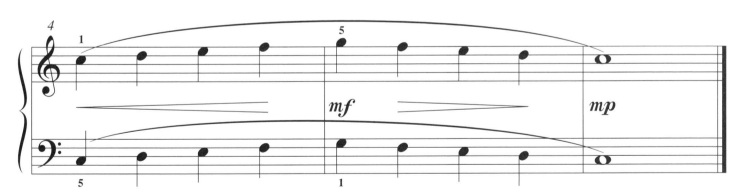

Note: Use this technique when playing on the white keys.

ETUDE

from *The Elementary Instruction Book, Variation 11*

Ferdinand Beyer
(1803-1863)

- For both etudes below, transfer the weight of your arm from one finger to the next finger as you move from key to key.

Moderato

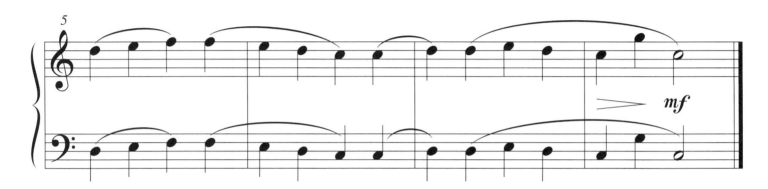

ETUDE

from *The Elementary Instruction Book, Variation 12*

Ferdinand Beyer
(1803-1863)

Moderato

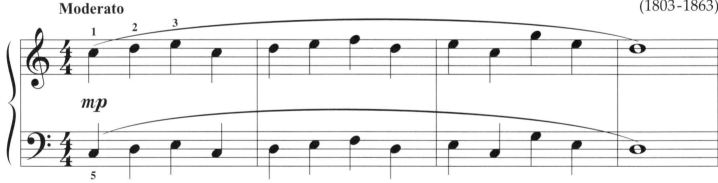

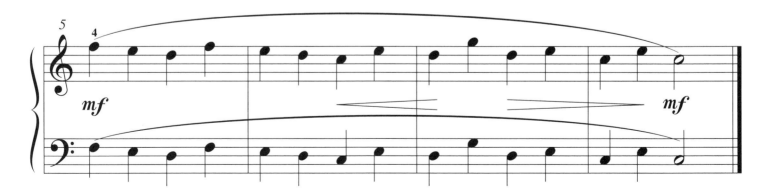

Transpose to: D major_____

G major_____

ETUDE

Daniel Gottlob Türk
(1750-1813)

- Practice hands separately before practicing hands together.
- Practice the right hand louder than the left hand. Then practice the left hand louder that the right hand. Which do you like better?

Allegro

ETUDE

from *The First Steps of the Young Pianist, Opus 82, No. 8*

Cornelius Gurlitt
(1820-1901)

- Notice when the hands are moving in the same direction.

Moderato

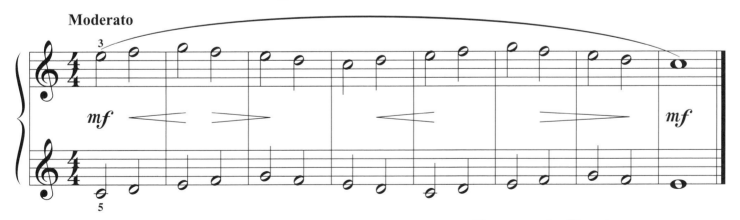

Transpose to: D major_____

G major_____

A major_____

Unit 4 - Two Friends Walking (Two-Part Counterpoint)

Many pieces have a melody in one hand, and the harmony in the other hand. But there are also other kinds of pieces you will play. These have a single-line melody in the right hand, and a single-line melody in the left hand, played at the same time.

Here are two kinds of counterpoint:

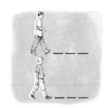

Mirror Pieces

For every important note in the right hand, there is an equally important note in the left hand. Imagine two friends mirroring each other, as they walk along.

Helen Marlais

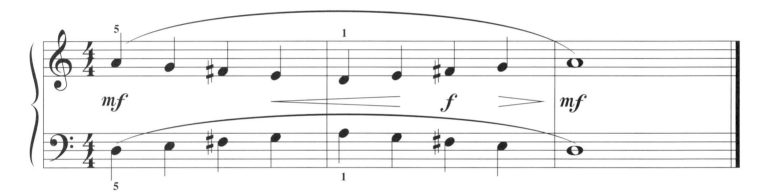

Imitation

When one friend walks, the other is one step behind, but completely in sync. In music, when one hand plays, the other hand imitates, or repeats what the other hand plays. The two melodies overlap.

Helen Marlais

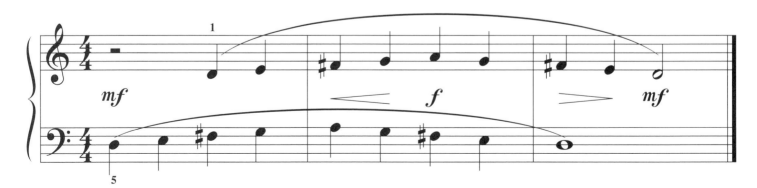

ETUDE

from *The First Steps of the Young Pianist, Opus 82, No. 12*

Cornelius Gurlitt
(1820-1901)

- Notice how one hand "imitates" what the other hand plays in both of these etudes.

ETUDE

(Opus 101, No. 22)

Ferdinand Beyer
(1803-1863)

- Before playing, tap the piece hands together while counting aloud.

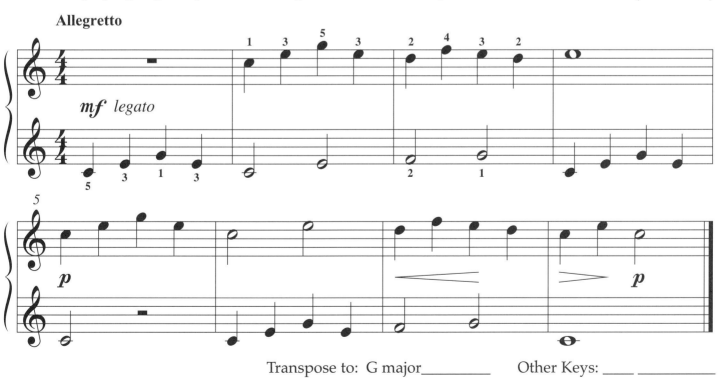

Transpose to: G major_____   Other Keys: ____ _____

D major_____   ____ _____

Four Etudes

Timothy Brown
(1959-   )

- Notice how every note in the right hand has a corresponding note in the left hand that is equally important.

No. 1

No. 2

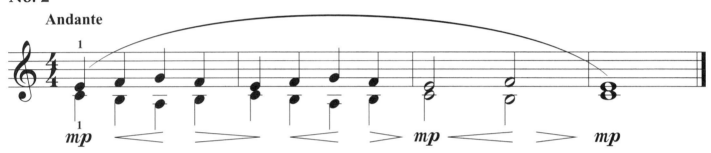

No. 3

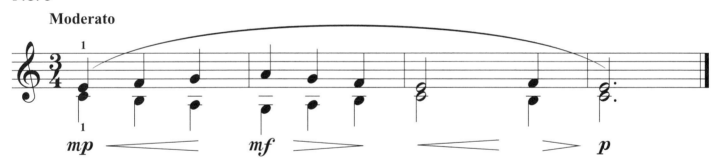

No. 4

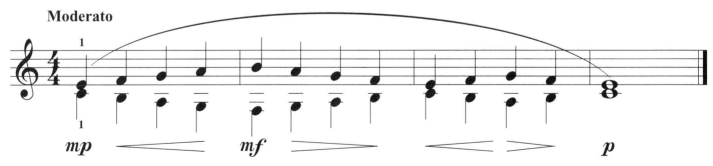

CANON IN F
(Opus 14, No. 9)

Konrad Max Kunz
(1812-1875)

- Mark the form in the music. Is it AA or AB?
- Practice in small sections: One measure plus one beat, and then two measures plus one beat.

Andante

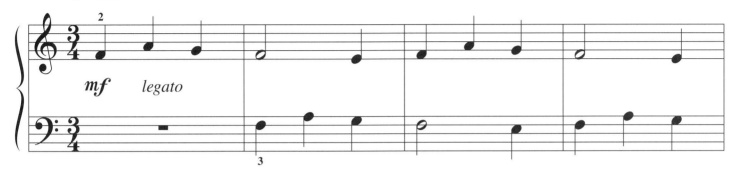

Prairie Moon

Valerie Roth Roubos
(1955-   )

- Notice where the intervals of a third are.
- In the right hand, drop your hand and arm to the bottom of the key when playing with your thumb. Then, roll your hand and arm to your fifth finger. Your hand and arm will reach its highest point when playing with the fifth finger.

ABOUT THE COMPOSERS

Johann Christian Bach, (1735-1782) and Francesco Pasquale Ricci, (1732-1817)

Johann Christian was the youngest son of the great composer, Johann Sebastian Bach. His father and an older brother taught him how to play the keyboard and he became a skilled musician, just like the rest of his family members. When he was 19 years old, he went to Italy to study opera. In 1778-79, Johann met Pasquale Ricci—an Italian composer and choirmaster—and together they wrote a piano method. The pieces in this method prepare students for the music of Haydn and Mozart.

Ferdinand Beyer, (1803-1863)

This German composer and pianist wrote a very popular piano teaching method that is still used today in some countries. You will find quite a few of his pieces in this book that, if practiced correctly, will help you become a better pianist.

Timothy Brown, (b. 1959)

Timothy Brown has written over 100 compositions for piano, as well as for orchestra, choir, ballet, chamber ensemble, and harpsichord. Many of his works have garnered significant awards and reviews. He is currently a fine arts specialist for the Dallas Public Schools.

Carl Czerny, (1791-1857)

This pianist, composer, and historian was one of Beethoven's pupils and later became a famous piano teacher in Vienna, Austria. He started teaching piano at the age of fifteen and composed nearly 1,000 works!

Cornelius Gurlitt, (1820-1901)

Gurlitt wrote many pieces for the piano, especially for young children. He was born in Germany and lived in Denmark and Italy. Then he returned to Germany and became a military bandmaster.

Konrad M. Kunz, (1812-1875)

Born in a city in Bavaria, Germany, Konrad Kunz was a student of theology and music in the historic city of Amberg, then a composer and teacher in Munich. He is known as the composer of the Bavarian national hymn. He wrote 200 canons for the piano. These are studies in using the hands independently. The lines of each hand move in parallel and contrary motion throughout.

Helen Marlais, (b. 1965)

Marlais' critically acclaimed and award-winning piano series, *Succeeding with the Masters*®, *The Festival Collection*®, *In Recital*®, as well as the rest of the *The FJH Pianist's Curriculum* by Helen Marlais, are designed to motivate and guide students to succeed as pianists and musicians for a lifetime of enjoyment in music. As a classical pianist, she has performed extensively throughout the U.S., Canada, Europe, and Asia; and is recorded on Gasparo, Centaur, and Stargrass Records. Dr. Marlais is an Associate Professor of Music at Grand Valley State University in Michigan, and is the coordinator of the piano performance and piano pedagogy programs.

Valerie Roth Roubos, (b. 1955)

Valerie Roth Roubos earned degrees in music theory and composition, and flute performance from the University of Wyoming. Ms. Roubos maintains a studio in her home in Spokane, Washington, where she teaches flute, piano, and composition. Her teaching philosophy and compositions reflect her belief that all students, from elementary to advanced, are capable of musical playing that incorporates sensitivity and expression.

Daniel Gottlob Türk, (1750-1813)
Türk was from Germany and made important contributions to the musical life there. He was not only a composer, but also a violinist and organist. He wrote an important method that was used during that time.